HISTORY'S
VILLAINS

KIM
IL SUNG

Scott Ingram

BLACKBIRCH®
PRESS

THOMSON
GALE

San Diego • Detroit • New York • San Francisco • Cleveland • New Haven, Conn. • Waterville, Maine • London • Munich

LIBRARY OF CONGRESS CATALOGING-IN-PUBLICATION DATA

Ingram, Scott (William Scott)
  Kim Il Sung / by Scott Ingram.
      v. cm. — (History's villains)
  Includes bibliographical references and index.
  Contents: Early years — Bandit and officer — The Korean conflict — The brain of the people — Tension and violence — Failure in the final years.
   ISBN 1-4103-0259-8
   1. Kim, Il-sæong, 1912—Juvenile literature. 2. Heads of state—Korea (North)—Biography—Juvenile literature. 3. Korea (North)—History—Juvenile literature. I. Title. II. Series.

  DS934.6.K6I54 2004
  951.9304'3'092—dc21

                                                                  2003010682

Printed in the United States
10 9 8 7 6 5 4 3 2 1

CONTENTS

Introduction:
"We Must Wipe Out
the Traitors"

In June 1953, ten of the highest-ranking officers in the Korean armed forces were marched to the central square of Pyongyang, the nation's capital. The men were blindfolded, and their arms were tied behind their backs at the elbow with wire. In front of a large crowd, the officers were forced to kneel, and, one by one, were shot in the back of the head. The bodies were dumped into a truck and carted away. Most of the onlookers believed the men were traitors who were responsible for North Korea's failure to achieve victory in a disastrous three-year war. Many were convinced the men deserved to die.

Death was no stranger to North Korea in 1953. War had torn apart the Korean peninsula for three years before the executions. Ten deaths meant little compared to the more than 3 million who had died in the brutal conflict between North and South Korea that North Korea began in an effort to unify the peninsula under one government. By 1953, the two nations had fought to a stalemate, and each had withdrawn to positions on either side of the 38th parallel. Millions of Korean soldiers and civilians were dead. Both countries had been devastated. Instead of unification, the war had brought ruin to both Koreas and the rest of the world to the edge of nuclear war.

Kim Il Sung wanted to unite North Korea and South Korea as a single Communist state.

The fighting had begun on June 25, 1950, when the leader of North Korea, Premier Kim Il Sung, had sent the North Korean army across the 38th parallel, a line that divided Communist North Korea from democratic South Korea. North Korean tanks, built in the Soviet Union, swept south in a wave of destruction. The next morning, Kim made a radio address to the people of North Korea. He spoke from his palace in Pyongyang. For the thirty-eight-year-old leader, this war was the final step in transforming all of Korea into a Communist state. The war was necessary, he told the nation, because the South Koreans had attacked first: "Dear brothers and sisters! Great danger threatens our motherland . . . and its people! We must wipe out the traitors in the South . . . [and] create a . . . democratic state! The war which we are forced to wage is a just war . . . for freedom and democracy."[1]

In fact, the South Koreans had not attacked; North Korea had. Kim had wanted to attack for several years.

5

Under Kim's orders, the North Korean army invaded South Korea on June 25, 1950. Kim, however, told his country that the South Koreans had attacked first.

It was a move, however, that could not have been made without the approval of the Soviet Union, the enormous Communist dictatorship that had funded North Korea's recovery from decades of colonization and war. Kim, who had gained fame as a tough guerrilla leader in World War II, had already led his country into deep financial debt to the Soviet Union and its dictator, Joseph Stalin. To conquer South Korea, Kim needed Soviet arms and equipment to supply his army—and he needed Stalin's permission.

Stalin, however, had been reluctant to launch a war that might involve the forces of his main enemy, the United States. For his part, Kim did not believe the United States would enter the war because the Americans had ended their occupation of South Korea in 1949.

Sensing Stalin's reluctance, Kim suggested that if Moscow did not help, he would turn to the other Communist giant on North Korea's border, China, which was led by Mao Tse-tung. In January 1950, Kim told Stalin's representative that if the Russians would not help unify Korea, "Mao Zedong is [my] friend and will always help Korea."[2]

The mention of Mao was the final straw. Kim knew Stalin regarded North Korea as a valuable source of minerals needed to develop atomic weapons and China would interfere with the Soviets' access to those minerals. In addition, Stalin believed that Mao had developed a type of communism that put China at odds with the Soviets.

Despite deep misgivings, Stalin permitted the South Korean invasion. Three years later, the war had ruined North Korea. Nevertheless Kim was determined to remain in control. He knew he needed to focus the blame on someone else, so he trumped up false charges of treason against the leaders of his army. The men were found guilty and sentenced to death at Kim's insistence.

When the officers were executed in 1953, Kim was among the many people who believed they should die. In truth, however, he knew that the men were not guilty of the crimes for which they been tried. They had to die to preserve his hold on power. That power grew over the last half of the twentieth century and made Kim one of the centurys' most dominating dictators. Millions more North Koreans died while Kim maintained his ruthless grip on the government, and the nation he ruled became one of the most isolated, poverty-stricken, and desperate countries in the world.

CHAPTER 1

EARLY YEARS

During the twentieth century, several nations were ruled by leaders who wielded absolute power. Some of them are notorious for the destruction and terror they caused. Adolf Hitler, for example, ruled Germany for only about twelve years but is largely responsible for starting World War II, which resulted in the deaths of an estimated 50 million people.

Some of these dictators controlled large countries for long periods, and their actions also resulted in enormous devastation. Among these tyrants was Joseph Stalin, who controlled the former Soviet Union for

Opposite: This giant bronze statue of Kim Il Sung is one of more than thirty thousand in North Korea that commemorate that country's leader.

Dictator Mao Tse-tung led Communist China for more than twenty-five years.

more than twenty years. Mao Tse-tung dominated China for more than twenty-five years. Both men played roles in millions of deaths.

One man remained in power longer than Hitler, Stalin, and Mao. North Korea's Kim Il Sung started a war that killed millions and brought the world to the brink of nuclear holocaust. He ruled North Korea for more than forty years.

Many North Koreans considered Kim the father of their nation. He was known to his people as "Great Leader," and by the time of his death, there were more than thirty thousand statues of him throughout the country. Like most tyrants, Kim was also feared by those he ruled. Unlike that of many dictators, however, his power never faltered, and even after his death, he remains a powerful force in the country that he ruled for so many years.

An Isolated Land

North Korea occupies the northern portion of the Korean peninsula, which is northwest of Japan and bordered by two of the largest nations in the world. China and Russia. This location made the Korean

peninsula, which was
divided into North
and South Korea at
the end of World War
II, a crossroads of
twentieth-century
history.

At roughly forty-
seven thousand square
miles, North Korea is
about the size of
Mississippi. More than
80 percent of the
land is mountainous,
and the rest is made
up of deep valleys
with occasional flat
plains. North Korea
has been one of the
most isolated countries
in the world since it
was founded in 1945.
Travel to it is extremely
difficult because only
two airlines fly into its

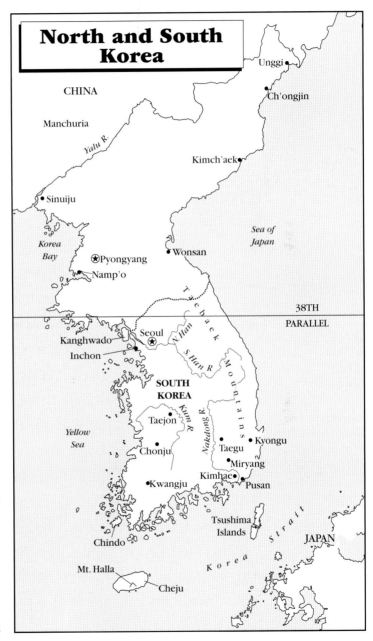

North and South Korea

CHINA

Manchuria

Yalu R.

Sinuiju

Korea Bay

Unggi

Ch'ongjin

Kimch'aek

Sea of Japan

Wonsan

Pyongyang

Namp'o

38TH PARALLEL

Seoul

Kanghwado

Inchon

N. Han R.

S. Han R.

T a e b a e k   M o u n t a i n s

SOUTH KOREA

Yellow Sea

Taejon

Kum R.

Nakdong R.

Chonju

Taegu

Kyongu

Miryang

Kimhae

Kwangju

Pusan

Tsushima Islands

Korea Strait

JAPAN

Chindo

Mt. Halla

Cheju

capital, Pyongyang, and there are few railways or paved roads that connect North Korea with its neighbors. Much of what occurs in the country is, according to journalist and historian Don Oberdorfer, "obscured in a secrecy that is unique in the world for its thoroughness."[3]

Because of this secrecy, many facts about Kim have been hidden from historians, and other facts about him have been wildly exaggerated. For example, in his autobiography and in books about him by North Koreans, he is depicted as a superhero who was capable of such magical feats as riding a leaf across a river to escape his enemies. Few North Koreans would question the truth of such a story, because for them, the "Great Leader" was a larger-than-life figure.

What is known about Kim is that he was born on April 15, 1912, in the village of Mangyongdae, near Pyongyang. He was born with the name Kim Song-ju and was the eldest of the three sons of Kim Hyong-jik and Kang Pan-sok. One of his brothers, Ch'ol-ju, was killed in World War II, but the other, Yong-ju, lived until the mid-1970s. Their father had a small farm, and he also sold herbal medicines. Both of their parents grew up in families that had converted to Christianity in the nineteenth century under the influence of European missionaries.

Under Japanese Occupation

The missionary influence was largely absent from Korea when Kim was born. In fact, there was little outside influence from any Western nation. Korea at that time had been an independent nation for thousands of years and was closed off and enslaved.

The reason for the country's isolation was that its mountains, which contained iron ore and coal, two valuable resources needed for making steel and a key element of industrial and military growth, made Korea attractive to invaders. The country's proximity to both Russia, which had cities and ports on the Pacific Ocean, and Japan, an island nation that had few natural resources, invited their attention as well by 1904, Russian troops had forced their way into Manchuria, a region north of Korea that had been governed by a weak government in China. Russian forces then marched south and took control of the Korean peninsula.

Japan strongly objected to these events, mostly because it, too, wanted control of Korea. The Japanese asked Russia to divide the peninsula. When the Russians refused the request, the Japanese navy attacked Russian naval bases in Asia. This conflict is known as the Russo-Japanese War. Within a year, Japan had taken control of a number of Russian ports on the Pacific coast.

The war between Russia and Japan erupted because both countries wanted control of the Korean peninsula. This painting depicts the Japanese navy firing on Russian forces.

The war, which ended in 1906, was finally settled when the United States persuaded both nations to attend a peace conference. Before the conference began, however, the United States signed a secret agreement with Japan that gave control of all of Korea to Japan in return for its agreement not to interfere with a U.S. takeover of the Philippines.

At the U.S.-led peace conference, the Russians agreed to leave Korea in return for the Japanese withdrawal from Russian naval bases. By 1912, when Kim was born, Korea was a colony of Japan.

The Japanese changed the entire society of Korea. For centuries, it had been ruled by an elite class, the *yangban*, made up of men who were scholars, government officials, and military officers. The *yangban* controlled large areas of land and pledged loyalty to the king, who ruled from the Korean capital of Seoul.

When Japan took control of Korea, it assigned a resident-general to oversee the military forces in the country. When the Korean king Kojon died in 1908, the resident-general assumed his powers. Although some local Korean militias took up arms against the Japanese, they had little effect.

In 1910, a wealthy and powerful Japanese business class came to Korea to replace the *yangban*. Japanese banks and industries took economic control of Korea. The Japanese used Korean peasants as slaves and forced them to build factories, railway lines, and roads. They also took the food grown on Korean farms and fed workers in the cities with it, which created famine conditions in much of rural Korea.

During Kim's childhood, Japanese businessmen forced small farmers off their land, bought the land at a low price set by Japanese bankers, then hired back the former farmers to work the land at extremely low wages. In this way, the Japanese were able to gain control of more than 20 percent of Korea's farmland. The land not under direct ownership of businesses was controlled by the Japanese government through brutal army officials who supervised peasant labor on the land. Protest was useless because Japanese courts enforced new laws that supported racial discrimination against Koreans. Eventually, Japanese replaced Korean as the national lanquage, and Koreans were forced to accept Shinto, the national religion of Japan. The loss of their culture was deeply humiliating for the Koreans.

Migration to Manchuria

Many Koreans who were enraged about Japan's policies were people who had once been *yangban*. In 1919, some of them appealed to Japan's emperor for Korean independence. His refusal to consider the request set off months of protests in Seoul, Pyongyang, and other Korean cities. The *yangban* and peasants both participated in the protests, which were ruthlessly crushed by the Japanese authorities. Hundreds of Koreans were publicly tortured and executed afterward for their roles in the uprising.

Although the independence movement failed, it created a strong spirit of nationalism among some Koreans, many of whom left the country. Many Korean Christians and members of the *yangban* formed a government in exile in Shanghai, a city in southern China. A large number of poor Koreans in the north could not afford to travel there and instead fled north across the Yalu

When the Russo-Japanese War ended, Japanese soldiers occupied Korea. Under Japan's military rule, Korea underwent dramatic changes in its economy, religious life, and even language.

River into the region of northern China known as Manchuria.

Among the poor families who fled was Kim's, who left Korea in 1920 when he was eight years old. Kim's father, who had joined a nationalist political organization, had been briefly imprisoned during the anti-Japanese demonstrations. To provide a better environment for his children and to improve his economic status, he moved his family to frigid Manchuria and opened an herbal medicine shop.

In his autobiography, written in the 1950s, Kim describes his family, and although he exaggerates aspects of his adult life, most historians agree that his description of his childhood is accurate. "Ours was a farm family.... We were honest, hardworking, poor farmers. One thing different about us was that we were passionately patriotic, willing to die for our country,"[4] he wrote.

Although Manchuria had long been part of China, the hundreds of thousands of Koreans who emigrated there met little resistance as they flooded into the province. At that time, China was in the initial stages of a civil war. For thousands of years, China's emperors held absolute control across the enormous country through a class system that was similar to Korea's *yangban*. In the last half of the nineteenth century, however, Western powers had taken control of some areas of China, and the emperor had been powerless to drive them out.

By the early 1900s, the emperor was little more than a figurehead, and the nation had split into numerous regions that were under the control of warlords. The Guomindang Party, a nationalist movement that sought a freer, more democratic government, had arisen and fought a war against the emperor's army. Because of the war and other problems facing China, nobody contested the entry of hundreds of thousands of Koreans into the northern province of Manchuria, which was distant from the turmoil in Beijing.

Kim attended Chinese school in Linjiang, Manchuria. As a young boy, he hated having to learn to learn a foreign language in addition to his other studies. By the time he was a teenager, however, Kim was glad he had gone to a Chinese school. In his autobiography, Kim wrote, "I did not know why Father had me enrolled in Chinese schools and made me learn Chinese at the time, but . . . my fluency in Chinese helped me."[5]

Rise of Communism

The political upheaval that took place in both China and Russia in the 1920s, while Kim was in school, had a lasting effect on Korea. The 1920s was the decade in which communism, a political philosophy in which there is no private property, spread around the globe. The philosophy is based on the writings of Karl Marx, a German philosopher. In his book *The Communist Manifesto*, written in 1848, Marx predicted that the workers of the world would eventually rebel against capitalists—wealthy owners of business and industry—and create a worldwide, classless society. A Communist government, according to Marx's theory, would own all business, industry, and agriculture, and would make all decisions in regard to the economy.

The first government based on the principles of communism had come to power in Russia in 1917.

Russia, the largest nation in the world, had borders on the Baltic Sea in the west and the Pacific Ocean in the east. The huge country had been ruled for centuries by czars, whose powers were absolute. Most of the Russian people lived in extreme poverty under the control of brutal government police. When World War I began in 1914, Russia was drawn into a massive conflict that brought the nation to ruin and weakened the hold of the czar and the police on the Russian people.

By early 1917, military defeats, food shortages, and economic collapse led to rioting in the streets of the Russian city of Saint Petersburg. In March 1917, the Communists seized power and executed the czar and his family. During the next five years, millions of Russians died during what became known as the Red Terror, as the huge nation transformed itself from a backward kingdom to a Communist nation.

By 1922, the Communists were firmly in control of Russia and changed the name of the country to the Union of Soviet Socialist Republics—also known as the Soviet Union. By that time Communist ideology had found followers among the Korean exiles and Chinese students who had traveled to Russia to learn more about it.

In 1923, the Soviet Union sent military advisers to assist the Chinese Guomindang nationalists. By 1924, a

Chinese Communist Party, led by a librarian from Beijing named Mao Tse-tung, had split off from the Guomindang. Three years later, Mao had assembled an army of about ten thousand troops and controlled several southern Chinese provinces.

Meanwhile, Communist ideology had also found proponents among some of the exiled Koreans. The Korean Communist Party was established in 1925 in Manchuria. Kim joined the party in 1927, a year after his father died.

In 1917, Vladimir Lenin seized power in Russia to lead the first Communist government. Communism spread around the world in the 1920s.

THE ROOTS OF COMMUNISM

Communism was developed as an economic theory by the German philosopher Karl Marx in 1848. In his book *The Communist Manifesto*, Marx set down his theories of history, economics, and the development of political systems. Marx believed that human history was a struggle for economic power between the ruling class, which he called the bourgeois, and the working class, which he called the proletariat. Most societies, according to Marx, would follow a three-stage path of development. The first stage consists of a feudal society ruled by an aristocratic bourgeois and a proletariat of serfs. In a feudal state, the bourgeois are landlords, and the workers are peasants. In Korea before Japanese occupation, the *yangban* would be the bourgeois. The majority of Koreans were peasants who worked the land. A large percentage of their harvest was paid to the landlords. According to Marx, such a system allows the bourgeois to live off the efforts of others without having to work. This is an unfair system, Marx believed.

The second stage in Marx's theory is capitalism. In the capitalist stage, a class of tradesmen forms that is better off than the serfs but not as well off as the bourgeois. The landholding aristocrats in this stage are replaced by wealthy capitalists called bosses, who control industry and resources. This stage also bears some similarity to the colonization of Korea by Japan.

In the capitalist stage, the members of the proletariat are paid small sums, and the bosses do not work. In the second stage, there is another class, which is called the petit bourgeois and is made up of smaller capitalists who own stores and farmers who own small amounts of land. These people are in business for themselves and do their own work. Under Japanese occupation, the Koreans

On his deathbed, Kim's father had given him a pistol and pleaded with him to join the revolt against the Japanese. Like most Koreans, Kim felt a duty to honor who collaborated with the Japanese invaders could be thought of as the petit bourgeois. Many Koreans considered them to be traitors for their acceptance of Japanese control.

In the third stage, according to Marx, the proletariat revolts and overthrows the bosses. In this final stage, the bosses lose all of the wealth they acquired through the labor of others. In order to make an ideal society in which all people are equal, Marx argued, all property, wealth, and possessions should be controlled by the state. Everyone works for the state and receives equal compensation. For Marx, the third stage represented the perfect society.

Many of those who endorsed Marx's ideas believed that this perfect society would be attained by natural and peaceful progression. These people called themselves Socialists. Marx, however, did not believe the revolution would be peaceful. Instead, he thought revolutionaries called Communists would lead the struggle. He also believed that in certain circumstances, it was possible to bypass the second stage. Under the most oppressive conditions, such as those in early-twentieth-century Russia, China, and Korea, the proletariat would revolt violently and their societies would move directly from stage one to stage three.

In Karl Marx's perfect society, the state would control all wealth and property.

and obey his elders—in this case, his father. At some point, Kim's anti-Japanese feelings found an outlet in Communist activities. It is unclear from his autobiography

how he learned about communism, but he organized
fellow students at his school into the Young Communists
League in 1927, and his political activities resulted in his
expulsion from school. At age fifteen Kim had become
dedicated to the Communist ideology of a "worker's
revolution."

Kim was arrested by Chinese authorities in 1929 for
his political activities and spent a year in a Manchurian

Japanese forces invaded Manchuria in 1931 (pictured). Communist guerrillas from both China and Korea united to fight their common enemy.

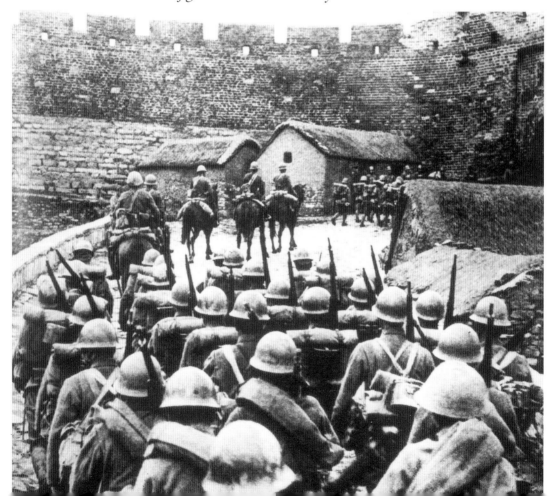

prison. At that time, the Guomindang controlled most of northern China and were extremely harsh with anyone who supported communism.

In 1931, however, the political differences between Chinese nationalists and Korean immigrants seemed unimportant compared with the fact that Japanese forces had invaded Manchuria. In effect, the invasion was a declaration of war on China. The Japanese took control of the region and renamed it Manchuko. Suddenly, Chinese and exiled Koreans were united in resistance. A scattered force of more than two hundred thousand Chinese and Korean guerrillas began to carry out hit-and-run raids against Japanese outposts. Among these groups was a band of Korean "bandits," as the Japanese called them, led by a young fighter who had taken the name Kim Il Sung in honor of a legendary fighter who had resisted Japanese attempts to conquer Korea several centuries earlier. This, of course, was the new name of Kim Song-ju, who was not yet twenty years old.

CHAPTER 2

BANDIT AND OFFICER

The fighting between the Japanese army and Communist guerrillas in Manchuria during the 1930s was fierce. Both sides used terror and torture to intimidate the other. Often, civilians, especially women and children, were caught in the fighting, and whole villages were sometimes destroyed. It was not unusual for guerrillas to come upon a village that had been attacked by the Japanese and find the severed heads of its residents displayed in the public square. It was also not unusual for Japanese troops to find the bodies of fellow soldiers who had been skinned alive or had ears, fingers, or other body parts cut off.

26

Guerrilla Actions

Kim and his small band operated in the rugged Chang Back mountain range, which straddled the border between Korea and Manchuria. There were a number of remote villages on the range that provided supplies and recruits. The number of Kim's troops ranged from about twenty to around three hundred.

Both men and women served with Kim's force, and although they supported Communist ideals, their

A photo shows Japanese soldiers as they confiscate the weapons of captured guerrillas. Kim Il Sung led a group of guerrilla bandits who fought along the border of Korea and Manchuria.

overwhelming passion was to defeat the Japanese and gain independence for Korea. In their efforts to recruit new fighters, the guerrillas realized that preaching Communist political theory to uneducated peasants was useless. Instead, Kim's followers talked about the peasants' hopeless poverty, landlords, and Japanese spies. They showed the peasants gruesome photos of atrocities committed on Koreans by the Japanese.

Kim's guerrillas also helped the peasants. They pitched in to harvest crops, collected firewood, and helped with other daily chores. At night, they entertained the younger peasants with stories of their bravery. Kim's stories of his exploits—both true and exaggerated—helped to make him one of the better-known guerrillas in the region.

Although they had only the bare necessities, the guerrillas needed money to pay for military supplies that they could not capture from the Japanese. Kim raised this money through extortion—he forced opium farmers in the region to pay him money in exchange for not destroying their crops.

A Reward on His Head

By 1935, Kim had become a big enough threat to the Japanese in Manchuria for them to offer a reward for his capture or death. Japanese guerrilla-fighting units were

Specialized Japanese units marched into Manchuria to fight the Communist guerrillas. In 1935, the Japanese targeted Kim as a threat and offered a reward for his capture or death.

formed to infiltrate the area, which led to an increase in atrocities. Japanese soldiers destroyed villages suspected of aiding Kim. They also set forest fires to destroy guerrilla hideouts. Anyone suspected of anti-Japanese activities was arrested, tortured, and executed.

None of this stopped Kim, who became even more widely known with a raid in Korea in the Japanese-controlled town of Pochonbo in 1937. The Korean guerrillas killed and mutilated fifty soldiers and captured a large supply of weapons. As a result of the Pochonbo raid, the Japanese raised the reward for Kim to ten thousand yen, a small fortune at the time.

Kim used extreme caution when he recruited new fighters, especially after he became a wanted man. Some recruits might be spies for the Japanese forces or eager to kill him for the reward, he feared. New recruits who were revealed to be Japanese sympathizers were tortured and killed, and Kim also ordered their entire families killed as a warning to anyone who tried to betray him.

Upheaval in China and Russia

Although Kim's fame rested mainly on his reputation as a bandit, he was a devoted follower of Communist principles. Those principles, however, changed in the 1930s when an ideological struggle took place in China and the Soviet Union.

In China, the conflict between the Guomindang and the Chinese Communists erupted into full-blown civil war in 1934. The Communists, who had control of the Jiangxi province in southeast China, were eventually surrounded by Guomindang forces led by Chiang Kai-shek. The fighting and a resulting famine led to the deaths of an estimated 1 million peasants in Jiangxi.

By October, the Communists realized they could no longer hold out against the larger Guomindang force. More than eighty thousand Communist soldiers set off on a six-thousand-mile march to western China. When they reached the security of the remote Shanxi province in northwestern China in the fall of 1935, more than 90 percent of them had died. The pursuit of the Communists across China had left much of the nation undefended, and Japan seized control of more Chinese territory.

The so-called Long March made Mao a legendary hero to Chinese Communists—and the Chinese who were under Japanese control admired Mao, rather than Chiang, whom they blamed for leaving China undefended. Mao had begun to see differences between the Soviet Communist theory and the communism that worked best in China. Like Kim in Manchuria, Mao realized that starving peasants had little interest in intellectual discussions. As he established a foothold in the mountains of Shanxi province, Mao wrote a

Overpowered by enemy Guomindang forces, Mao Tse-tung (left) and more than eighty thousand Communists marched six thousand miles across China in what is known as the Long March.

number of pamphlets that espoused a different style of communism from that of the Soviets.

Stalin's Rise

Meanwhile, traditional communism had also changed in the Soviet Union, largely because political power had fallen under the absolute control of one man. Like Kim and Mao, Iosif Vissarionovich Dzhugashvili came from a rural peasant background. Like both men, he had served time in prison for his beliefs. Like Kim, he had changed his name as he became more famous. He called himself Joseph Stalin—Stalin is Russian for "man of steel."

By the early 1930s, Stalin had established a dictatorship that ruled through propaganda, terror, and starvation. In an effort to modernize industry, he had forcibly relocated millions of citizens to Soviet cities. Farms were placed under government control and forced to send most of the food they grew to industrial areas. Stalin's policies resulted in mass starvation in some regions. It is estimated that 7 million people in one region, Ukraine, starved to death in the winter of 1932–1933.

In order to maintain control, Stalin ordered his secret police to spy on Soviet citizens, and those who spoke against Stalin's rule often ended up in the gulag—prison work camps. Fear ruled people's lives. Communist Party members were arrested if they did not clap at Stalin's speeches, for example Stalin signed more than 230,000 death warrants between 1934 and 1937.

Soviet citizens who disagreed with Stalin's government often ended up in prison camps like the one pictured here.

Of course, few people outside of the Soviet Union knew the truth about Stalin's brutality. State-controlled radio stations and newspapers extolled Stalin's heroic leadership. Communist groups around the world praised Stalin and the Soviet style of government. In his auto-biography, Kim wrote that "The Soviet [Union]...[is] the only type of government capable of putting an end to...exploitation and building...a free and peaceful new world."[6]

Flight to Siberia

Kim's view of Stalin was limited not only by Soviet propaganda, but also by his own relatively naive understanding of Communism. In 1940, Kim's main focus was on military action, despite his devotion to the Communist ideology. In this area, he had limited success. He led a force of 250 fighters against a Japanese antiguerrilla unit in the town of Daimalugou in northern Korea. The Koreans wiped out the larger unit, captured dozens of weapons, and publicly executed twenty captured prisoners. Throughout the fight against the Japanese, Kim searched local villages for criminals such as smugglers, thieves, and killers. (In his early rise to power, Stalin, too, used other criminals to further his agenda.) He would send them into Japanese-controlled areas to use their abilities to disrupt Japanese control.

Kim's military success, however, was minor and took place in a remote region. He did not drive the Japanese from Korea. In fact, by 1940, the Japanese military controlled most of China and Southeast Asia. In Korea and Manchuria, Japan's antiguerrilla campaigns began to take their toll. There were fewer recruits willing to live on wild plants and birds' eggs in the mountains, and fewer still were willing to risk their lives.

In late 1940, Kim and twenty-five or so guerrillas fled to Siberia, in the remote eastern region of the Soviet

Union. There they met other guerrillas who also had left Manchuria. At the time, the Soviets had a policy of neutrality toward Japan, and most of their armed forces were in the European region of the country, busy in the preparation defenses against a possible invasion by Nazi Germany.

The Soviets united Kim, his men, and squads of other Chinese, Koreans, and Soviet Asians into the 88th Special Independent Guerrilla Brigade of the Soviet army. Kim was given an officer's commission in the Soviet army and placed in command of a two-hundred-man battalion. He used his ability to speak both Korean and Chinese to his advantage, since most of the men spoke just one of the two languages. He soon acquired a basic knowledge of Russian, which made him an even more valued officer to the Soviets because he could translate their orders to the troops.

The brigade's initial duty was to sneak into Manchuria to gather intelligence about any Japanese attempts to take over parts of Russia's Pacific coast. This did not require many troops. In truth, Stalin and the Soviet command hoped to use the brigade's troops as an Asian Communist force when the war ended. Although he was supremely confident in his abilities, Kim was not as skilled a commander of a battalion as he was of a few dozen men. The missions he led into Manchuria ended in disaster.

In two trips across the border, Kim lost dozens of men under his command, who were captured by the Japanese and tortured to death. Before he died, one of Kim's officers revealed to the Japanese the location of the Soviet guerrilla base in Siberia, and Kim was forced to retreat to remote reaches of the vast region to keep Japanese units at bay.

World War II

While minor conflicts between guerrilla units took place in a distant corner of Asia, military expansion by Japan, Germany, and Italy set the stage for World War II. The German invasion of Poland in 1939 had led to war between Germany, France, and Great Britain. Although the Soviet Union had signed a nonaggression pact with Germany, the Nazis violated it when they invaded the Soviet Union in June 1941. Finally, on December 7, 1941, the Japanese attacked the American naval base at Pearl Harbor, Hawaii. By the end of the year, the United States had joined the Allies—Great Britain, the Soviet Union, and the United States—in a war against Germany, Japan, and Italy, which were known as the Axis powers.

During 1941, Kim and his unit remained in Siberia, where he married Kim Jung Suk, a young woman who had fought with the Korean guerrillas for several years in

Kim Jung Suk fought with Korean guerrilla forces for six years before she married Kim Il Sung in 1941. Their son, Kim Jong Il, was born the following year.

Manchuria after she joined them in 1935 at age sixteen. Like most of the women guerrillas, she took on many jobs: cook, seamstress, spy, food gatherer, and fighter.

In Siberia, as in Manchuria, women fighters were considered the equal of men. They practiced shooting and learned skiing and parachute jumping. All women, whether married or single, slept in a separate barracks from the men. In February 1942, Kim Jung Suk gave birth to the couple's first child, a boy named Kim Jong Il. A second child, born three years later, died in a childhood accident. Kim Jung Suk died in 1949 from tuberculosis.

In late 1942, Kim left his wife and infant son to travel west with his battalion to fight with other Soviet units at Stalingrad. The Soviet army was near defeat and involved in a battle for the survival of the Soviet Union. The battle, which began in August 1942, was one of the bloodiest in history. About 1.3 million Soviet and 800,000 German soldiers lost their lives in the six-month engagement. When Kim arrived, the brutal Russian winter had set in. Having fought in subzero cold for years, he was hardened to such temperatures. The Germans, however, were not prepared to fight into winter and eventually surrendered. The Battle of Stalingrad was a turning point in the defeat of the Nazis.

By 1945, World War II was nearing an end. Italy had surrendered in 1943, and in May 1945, Germany did, too. Only the Japanese continued to fight, and American forces battled them on islands in the Pacific. In August, American bombers dropped atomic bombs on the Japanese cities of Hiroshima and Nagasaki. This first use of nuclear weapons killed hundreds of thousands of Japanese and brought the country to its knees.

By August 1945, it was clear Japan would soon surrender. Only then did Stalin declare war on Japan and send the Soviet army racing across Manchuria into Korea. During the final days of World War II, the decision was made to divide Korea, and it was made by the United States.

A Peninsula Divided

Although the Soviet Union was one of the Allies, few American leaders trusted Stalin, and most deeply disliked communism. When the Americans received word that Soviet troops were moving south across the Manchurian border, they realized they had to act or Stalin would control all of Korea. Before, the Americans had assumed that the nationalist Korean exiles in Shanghai would return to lead the country after the Japanese surrender. The unexpected news that Stalin's forces were entering Korea was unacceptable to the Americans, who suspected Stalin might try to extend Soviet power in Asia.

At a meeting in Washington, D.C., in August 1945, outside the presence of any Korean leaders, Colonel Dean Rusk, who was later secretary of state, drew a line across a map of Korea at the 38th parallel, between the country's two largest cities, Seoul and Pyongyang. The surrender agreement signed by Japan on August 16 included the provision that when the Japanese left Korea, American forces would occupy the country up to the 38th parallel. Soviet forces stopped their advance at that point.

There are no records of Kim's whereabouts during the final three months of World War II. By that time, most of the Korean officers who had joined the Soviets during the war had been killed. Kim was one of the few survivors.

At some point during that time, it is believed, Stalin made his choice to put Kim in charge of establishing a Communist government in Korea. Stalin is quoted as saying, "Korea is a young country, and it needs a young leader."[7]

After Korea was divided, the rugged mountain terrain along the 38th parallel (pictured) became the border between North and South Korea.

Hero's Welcome

In late September 1945, when Kim entered Pyongyang in a Soviet army officer's uniform, thousands of Koreans lined the streets to cheer him. The thirty-three-year-old guerrilla leader had been fighting the Japanese for more than fifteen years. His exploits as a bandit were well known among the Koreans, and despite his youth and his lack of political experience, he had no doubt that he was the right person to lead the Korean people out of the disaster of World War II. Kim described the scene in his autobiography:

> Standing on the platform amidst the enthusiastic cheers of more than 100,000 people, I felt happiness that defied description. . . . It was happiness . . . from the feeling that the people loved and trusted me. . . . My speech that day . . . appealed to the whole nation to build a prosperous, independent state in Korea. . . . The crowd expressed [its] support with thunderous applause and cheers.[8]

Kim left little doubt about what his role would be in North Korea. In early October, Kim, who had never finished high school, had Pyongyang University

THE COLD WAR

At the end of World War II, the Soviet Union occupied nine Eastern European countries as well as half of Germany. The influence of communism had also spread into Asia, as was evidenced by the rise to power of China's Mao Tse-tung and Kim Il Sung in Korea. Stalin used terror tactics to exert control on the occupied nations. Under Stalin, they were ruled by Communist leaders who were loyal to Stalin, and their economies were linked to the Soviet Union's. If Communist control was threatened, their armies or secret police—or the Soviets'—were used to stamp out the insurrection.

Joseph Stalin's declaration that capitalism was incompatible with communism helped lead the Soviet Union into the Cold War.

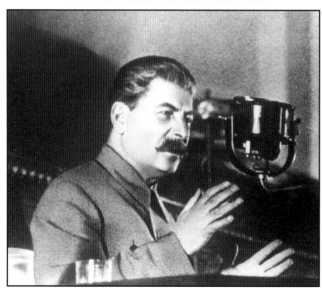

In February 1946, Stalin gave a speech in which he declared that communism and capitalism were incompatible. Around the same time, an American diplomat in Moscow wrote a memo in which he called communism a danger to the free world.

These events and others like them began what became known as the Cold War, a term that was coined by British author George Orwell in 1945 and refers to a conflict between nations that involves extreme tension despite the absence of all-out war. Orwell wrote two novels—*Animal Farm* and *1984* in the 1940s—that criticized the Soviet Union and other nations controlled by one person or party.

Tensions between the United States and the Soviet Union increased in the 1940s as both sides developed nuclear weapons. The United States invented and first used atomic bombs in World War II. The Soviet Union successfully exploded a test weapon in August 1949. The Cold War cast a dark shadow over the world after World War II, and nowhere was that shadow darker than on the Korean peninsula, where the two sides ended up facing each other across the 38th parallel.

renamed Kim Il Sung University. He then declared that only the sons and daughters of peasants, workers, and revolutionary soldiers could attend the school.

In February 1946, a people's committee led by Kim and 160 of his guerrilla comrades became the young nation's first central government. The following month, land reform was instituted, and all private lands were seized by the government without payment to the owners. Kim accused owners who objected of having aided the Japanese—virtually a death sentence. The peasants, whom Kim had convinced would benefit from land reform, formed vigilante groups. Mobs attacked and killed thousands of landholders who sought to reclaim land they owned before the Japanese invasion in the early twentieth century.

CHAPTER 3

THE KOREAN CONFLICT

Although Kim spoke to North Koreans about building a single, independent state, he closely followed the example of the leader he most admired, Stalin. During Stalin's rise to power, he always found groups to blame for any problems that arose. Kim, of course, had the Japanese to find fault with for the terrible conditions in Korea after the war. He used the anti-Japanese feeling to turn peasants and others against landholders and former members of the *yangban*. There were many vigilante killings by peasant mobs in the early years of Kim's rule.

Birth of North Korea

For much of 1946, North Koreans looked to Kim for direction despite the facts that he had never commanded more than three hundred people and that he had never handled the detailed responsibilities of running a nation. Nevertheless, he pushed to bring about a Communist government modeled on his understanding of Stalin's rule. Members of the rapidly growing North Korean Workers' Party took control of private farms and killed Koreans who were said to have helped the Japanese. To increase the power of the single party, Kim prohibited nationalists and Christian leaders from participating in politics.

Kim also adopted a plan similar to the one used in the Soviet Union in the 1930s to rapidly increase industrialization. Soviet propaganda made the plan seem as though it had miraculously changed the agricultural Soviet economy into a modernized, industrial economy. In truth, it had failed. Nationalized major Korean industries that had previously been managed by their technically advanced Japanese owners were

A postcard shows a Soviet worker holding a copy of Joseph Stalin's "Five-Year Plans". Kim implemented a similar plan to increase the industrialization of Korea.

45

suddenly in the hands of inexperienced Korean Communist Party members. Following a two-year plan based on Stalin's model, Kim relied on the skills of his former comrades to oversee an economy based on heavy industry, which included the manufacture of trucks, tractors, and large industrial machines.

Birth of South Korea

While Kim formed a Communist government in North Korea, the new nation south of the 38th parallel was also growing its economy, undergoing changes. For three years after World War II, more than twenty-five thousand American troops had occupied South Korea while the nationalists returned to Seoul and attempted to establish a democratic government. The Americans found themselves surrounded by a Korean population that, after its country's long occupation, was deeply suspicious of foreigners. Various nationalist groups insisted that South Koreans were ready to govern themselves in a democratic manner, despite having no experience doing so.

During South Korea's transition from occupied colony to independent nation between 1945 and 1948, the U.S.-educated Syngman Rhee began to assert his influence. Although Rhee claimed he wanted democracy

Syngman Rhee, the first president of the Republic of South Korea, enjoyed strong support from the United States because of his anti-Communist stance.

in South Korea, he was considered by many Koreans to be a *yangban* who wanted absolute control. Nevertheless, he had American support because of his strong anti-Communist beliefs, and in 1948, Rhee was elected as the first president of the Republic of South Korea. The U.S. military commander in the Pacific, General Douglas MacArthur, believed that the South Korean army was strong enough to defend itself without American support and, in 1949, American troops were withdrawn from Korea.

Mao's Victory

While Americans were leaving the Korean peninsula, important events that would affect the entire region

47

were taking place in China. Almost as soon as the Japanese were defeated and driven from China, the battle between Chiang Kai-shek's nationalist Guomindang and Mao's Communist forces resumed. American forces, which had occupied parts of China at the end of World War II, were withdrawn for fear of being drawn into the conflict. Instead, the United States gave economic aid to Guomindang forces.

Although they had economic support from the United States, the Guomindang had little popular support. Many Chinese bitterly recalled that Chiang's pursuit of the Communists into western China in the 1930s had left the nation undefended against Japanese invasion and conquest. As a result, although the Guomindang had more troops and more modern weaponry, the Communist forces controlled most of the north and northeastern areas of the country by late 1948.

In January 1949, the Communists took control of Beijing, the Chinese capital. Throughout the winter and spring, city after city fell to the Communists. In June, the Guomindang army fled China and went to the island of Taiwan. On October 1, 1949, the People's Republic of China, under the control of Chairman Mao Tse-tung, was founded. In December, Chiang proclaimed Taipei, Taiwan, the temporary capital of Nationalist China.

The People's Republic of China was formed after the Communists took control of cities all across China.

Power Expands

As Mao's hold on China intensified, Kim focused on strengthening his own grip on power. Like Stalin, he named himself the secretary of the Communist Central Committee, the nation's only political party. As its leader, Kim appointed supporters to positions of power, and they, in turn, carried out his orders. The party's hold on the people was total. Party officials were placed in businesses, factories, government offices, military units, and schools. In villages, party officials formed committees to supervise state-controlled farms.

Kim and his followers had general public support. Their support, however, came less from communism's

THE COMMUNISM OF CHAIRMAN MAO

Mao Tse-tung believed that the Communist revolution in China should begin among peasants in the countryside.

China and Russia developed differing interpretations of how communism should be put into practice. Early Russian Communists believed that the final struggle before communism became the world's ruling political model would take place between workers and capitalist bosses. Russian Communists also thought that the revolution would begin in an urban, rather than rural, setting. As a result, the communism that developed in the Soviet Union depended upon the destruction of the peasant class.

To implement this, the Soviets forced peasants to form collective farms. All food grown on the collectives was taken from the peasants and given to industrial workers and party officials. Those policies resulted in the starvation of millions of peasants. In 1922 alone, 5 million died. For Soviet leaders, the death of uneducated peasants was insignificant compared to the survival of skilled workers and those who understood the Soviet theory of communism.

As the son of farmers, Mao, by contrast, believed in the revolutionary spirit of Chinese peasants, who had suffered for centuries under emperors and occupying nations. He believed revolution in China should begin in the countryside rather than in its cities. When the Chinese Communist Party was established in 1925, Soviet leaders considered China too backward to become a so-called people's republic. Soviet leaders told Mao that before they would financially assist the Chinese Communist Party, Mao had to work with the anti-Communist Guomindang to make China a more urban nation. This policy aroused a deep resentment in Mao and his followers that was never overcome and contributed to a split between the two Communist giants. Mao never gave up on his devotion to the peasants, whom he thought should be at the center of the revolution.

appeal than it did from Kim's exaggerated reputation as a fighter against the Japanese. North Koreans were told that Kim had led all Korean resistance against Japan. In truth, there had been many units acting separately in Manchuria. Many leaders were killed in fighting, however, and Kim's hardcore group of fighters were willing to use force against any of Kim rivals, on and off the battlefield.

Kim's following was also the result of his leadership style. Unlike the yangban, Kim went out among the people and visited factories and farms to give advice and encouragement. Like Mao, Kim believed that the peasants were the foundation of a Communist revolution.

Kim's faith in the masses differed from the communism practiced by Stalin. Nevertheless, Kim was extremely loyal to Stalin, and Kim's closest supporters regarded Stalin as their main influence as well. Their admiration of the Soviet Union did not go unnoticed. Many North Koreans wanted a truly independent North Korean nation and resented the leadership's devotion to the Soviet Union.

The Soviet's influence was especially strong among members of the secret police, as well as at radio stations and newspapers, all of which were staffed by Koreans who had spent years being educated in the Soviet Union. Kim's biggest challenge was not persuading the people that he was worthy of leadership—it was in gaining control of all the Communist splinter groups and molding them into a single party. In addition to his close guerrilla supporters, some Communists had remained in Korea during the colonial period and wished to be rewarded for their efforts. Other Koreans were more loyal to Chinese communism. Kim was suspicious of these groups, and in his quest for power, loyalty to him became more important than devotion to Communist ideology.

Because of Kim's desire for personal loyalty, he favored a group of North Koreans who had converted to communism at the same time Kim rose to power. These people were generally illiterate peasants and workers who did not understand communism and had joined the party in hopes of favorable treatment from the government. These were the Koreans who attacked the landholders accused of Japanese sympathies. The most ruthless among them were rewarded by Kim with key management jobs at businesses, factories, and farms. Although doing so helped Kim to solidify power, as managers, they had a disastrous effect on North Korea's economy.

Within a little more than two years, Kim had become a dictator in the mold of Stalin. He had a select group of loyalists who backed his every move, and had filled government and party posts with those who supported him and his style of communism. At the local level, he had given positions of authority to uneducated people who owed their livelihoods to his hold on power. Most important, he had absolute control over military and security forces. By 1948, when Kim was named premier of the Democratic People's Republic of Korea, Stalin was confident enough in Kim to order all Soviet troops and advisers out of the country.

War for the Korean Peninsula

A short time after Soviet troops left North Korea, more than eighty thousand Korean troops returned from the conflict in China. The return of these battle-tested troops to North Korea doubled the size of the army. This sudden expansion of his armed forces increased Kim's determination to invade South Korea and overthrow its government. The fact that U.S. forces had withdrawn also increased Kim's desire for war.

On New Year's Day 1950, Kim gave a radio speech that reached listeners on both sides of the 38th parallel. He encouraged South

In the early months of 1950, Kim readied to invade South Korea. To attain Stalin's help, Kim told the Soviet leader that North Korea could overthrow the South Korean government in just a few days.

Koreans to overthrow Rhee and promised the corrupt "errand boy" of the Americans would soon be "destroyed from within and without."[9]

Kim knew he could not invade South Korea without the permission of Stalin. Early in 1950, Kim traveled to Moscow to make his case for invasion. Kim lied and told Stalin that South Korean forces had made minor attacks across the 38th parallel and were massed for an all-out attack. He confidently predicted to Stalin that the North Korean army would defeat the South Koreans in a few days and that the Unites States would not have time to send troops to their rescue.

When Stalin continued to express doubts, Kim played his trump card and suggested that he would turn to China for economic and military assistance. This, Stalin feared, would cut off his access to North Korea's resources of tungsten and other minerals needed for the rapidly growing Soviet nuclear-weapons arsenal.

Eventually, Stalin bowed to Kim's wishes, but not before warning the North Korean leader that the Soviet Union could not divert troops from Eastern Europe to help him. Kim assured Stalin that no help would be necessary.

On June 25, 1950, North Korea launched a massive attack across the 38th parallel toward Seoul. More than ninety thousand North Korean troops, joined by more than

150 Soviet-supplied T-34 tanks, routed forward units of the South Korean army. As the North Korean force raced toward Seoul, thousands of wounded South Korean soldiers and fleeing civilians were killed when the enormous tanks drove over them and crushed them to death.

Within two days, the South Korean army had abandoned defenses around Seoul, and the roads that led south from the city were jammed with refugees and retreating South Korean troops. North Koreans fired long-range artillery into the fleeing masses, killing soldiers and civilians indiscriminately. In the first week of the war, more than thirty-four thousand South Korean troops, one-third of the South Korean army, had been killed or captured, or were missing.

The North Korean advance was so rapid that the advancing army had to pause for a week to allow gas, ammunitions, and other supplies to reach them. That delay allowed the South Korean army to reach the southern port city of Pusan, where they regrouped and joined twenty thousand American troops that had been rushed to South Korea from Japan. Once the North Koreans had been resupplied, they advanced toward Pusan.

The fighting around Pusan in the summer of 1950 was some of the most brutal of the Korean War. On August 24, a force of nearly ten thousand North Korean troops and twenty-five tanks launched an attack. Each side lost more than half its troops in bloody hand-to-hand fighting. Finally, the North Koreans were thrown back.

In Pyongyang, Kim was eager to prove to Stalin his prediction of a rapid defeat of the South Koreans. To create the atmosphere of terror that he felt was necessary to force surrender, he ordered his troops to execute all prisoners and kill any civilians who impeded their progress. As a result of Kim's order, North Korean troops killed untold thousands of soldiers and civilians indiscriminately. In one town, Taejon, North Koreans tied up and machine-gunned more than seven thousand civilians, South Korean soldiers, and American troops.

Kim directed his North Korean troops to employ guerrilla tactics against prisoners. The North Koreans obeyed, and tortured and mutilated prisoners. Dozens of American troops who were captured in fighting around Pusan had their feet cut off before they were shot, and had their eyes gouged out or tongues cut out before death. Mass executions took place regularly in which prisoners' hands were tied behind their backs with barbed wires and they were marched to open areas, where they were cut down by machine-gun fire.

While the Americans and South Koreans fought desperately to hold off the North Koreans, the newly formed United Nations sent a force made up of troops from several nations, including more troops from the United States, to reinforce Pusan. The additional forces included one key element that the North Koreans did not possess: air power. Heavy bombing by the U.S. Air Force kept the North Koreans from complete victory. For most of August, American bombers pounded North Korean military positions in the south, as well as Pyongyang and other North Korean cities.

Counterattack by MacArthur

By the end of August, the American commander in Korea, General Douglas MacArthur, had enough combined South Korean, American, and UN troops to counterattack. On September 15, the combined force landed at Inchon, a port on the west coast of Korea, near Seoul. This action cut the supply and communication lines of the North Korean army. Within days, the North Korean army had been pushed back behind the 38th parallel. On October 2, Kim, who so confidently predicted that victory would take days, was forced to ask Mao for help in a telegram: "[Enemy] forces attacking the area north of the 38th Parallel, our situation is extremely disadvantageous. Request Chinese Peoples Liberation Army be directly mobilized for us immediately."[10]

On October 19, 1950, Pyongyang fell to American forces, and Kim had fled the city. Civilians, this time North Koreans, were again caught in the fighting as they fled the city. Less than four months after North Korea's attack, its army had lost the majority of its tanks and large artillery in South Korea, and sixty thousand North Korean soldiers had been killed. Although Kim had reserve troops, the North Korean army was outnumbered and undersupplied.

General Douglas MacArthur's effective leadership of the combined UN, American, and South Korean forces led Kim to ask Mao and Stalin for military support in South Korea.

Mao, whose army had suffered through twenty-five years of war, was reluctant to put his troops into combat again so soon. He knew that airpower was needed for any chance of victory. He asked Stalin for air support, and he agreed to send two Soviet air force units to bases in Manchuria. He also agreed to provide transport trucks and ammunition for use by the Chinese. With these assurances from Stalin, Mao sent 250,000 troops across the Yalu River on November 1.

For the next two months, the North Korean and Chinese Communist forces pushed UN, U.S. and South Korean troops south in brutal, bloody fighting. The Chinese, armed with outdated weapons from World War I, attacked in human waves and overwhelmed the defenders. South Koreans and American soldiers killed thousands of Chinese, yet there were too many to stop.

In late November, at the key battle at the Chosin Reservoir in North Korea, American troops fought their way across frozen ice to escape encirclement. The forces fought in howling winds and temperatures of twenty below zero. Guns would not fire, vehicles froze, and thousands of soldiers on both sides died of exposure during the coldest winter in North Korea in two hundred years. The Americans were able to escape, but the retreat signaled the end of the attempt to defeat North Korea.

At the end of 1950, the North Koreans and Chinese retook Pyongyang, which had been bombed to ruins. Kim immediately relieved the senior commanders of his army of their duties and took direct control of the army. He also ordered the execution of hundreds of North Korean political prisoners who had spoken out against the war or against him. To make identification of the prisoners more difficult for their families, he directed police to pour acid over the bodies to disfigure them.

HOW CLOSE WAS NUCLEAR WAR?

At the outbreak of the Korean War, the United States had been a nuclear power for five years and the Soviets for little more than a year. Few people on either side, however, understood the enormous power of the weapons. Soviet leader Joseph Stalin, for example, frequently spoke about developing nuclear missiles for a war with the West. He was prepared to start such a conflict in order to achieve a worldwide Communist government only because he did not know that it would likely have destroyed much of the planet.

Americans, too, had little understanding of the awesome power of atomic weapons, even though they had been used against Japan. In 1951, when American commander Douglas MacArthur asked the defense department for twenty-six atomic bombs to drop across Manchuria, many Americans supported him. Few, of course, understood that they would wipe out life in much of Asia and lead to nuclear holocaust in the rest of the world. In the end, MacArthur's request was denied—the United States did not even have ten such bombs in its arsenal, let alone twenty-six. The Soviet Union, on the other hand, had more than twenty bombs, and each of them was twice as powerful as the biggest American bomb. In the end, the Korean War brought the world closer to nuclear holocaust than many people realized.

The Korean War brought the world to the edge of nuclear war.

A Prolonged Conclusion

In early January 1951, the killing continued when
North Korean and Chinese troops captured Seoul, the
second time the city had fallen to invaders. More than
two hundred thousand civilians in South Korea had been
killed in six months of fighting. News agencies reported
that MacArthur had requested a large number of atomic
bombs from the U.S. arsenal, and information was leaked

By the end of the Korean War, South Korea's capital city of Seoul (pictured) was in ruins.

that he planned to drop the bombs in Manchuria and create a wall of radioactivity to hold off the Chinese.

When Stalin was informed about McArthur's plan, he immediately stopped all assistance to North Korea and the Chinese. He did so because he had signed an agreement with China in 1949 that committed the Soviet Union to help defend China in the event of an attack, and he was unwilling to become involved in a war with the United States. Because of this, the Soviet air units were never used in the war, and badly needed supplies stopped flowing to North Korea. The sudden withdrawal of support infuriated Mao and created lifelong mistrust between Chinese and Soviet Communists. In addition, it forced the North Koreans and Chinese to withdraw behind the 38th parallel because they could not supply their troops.

In the end, Mao realized that continued fighting would gain little and could bring nuclear devastation. MacArthur's eagerness to use atomic weapons also alarmed the UN, and members of that body's security council increased pressure on both sides to end the bloodshed. By late winter, forces once again faced each other on opposite sides of the 38th parallel. Although occasional battles took place to gain a few miles of ground during the next two years, the major fighting

Heavy U.S. bombing helped South Korea push the North Korean forces back to the 38th parallel.

was over by the summer of 1951, a little more than a year after Kim had attacked. The Korean War ended where it began.

Kim's desire for conquest, however, had destroyed both countries. By July 1953, when the armistice was signed and a demilitarized zone (DMZ) established for two hundred meters on either side of the 38th parallel, North Korea had been reduced to rubble. An estimated 2 million to 3 million civilians had died—more than 10 percent of the Korean population. Families had been permanently separated by the 38th parallel, millions of children were orphaned, and millions more suffered from starvation. More than 1.5 million North Korean soldiers and 500,000 South Korean soldiers were killed. The economies of both countries were shattered. Not a single building was left standing in Pyongyang, and Seoul was also in ruins.

Personally, Kim had lost the confidence of Stalin, the man he looked up to as a hero. Although he immediately began to take steps to rebuild relations with the Soviet Union, it was too late to rebuild them with Stalin, who died from a stroke in May 1953.

CHAPTER 4

THE BRAIN OF THE PEOPLE

Almost as soon as the armistice was signed, Kim began to blame others for the disaster he had brought on North Korea. This was the same strategy used by Stalin during the 1930s, when he decided to arouse public opinion against the established leaders of the Communist Party. Anyone who could possibly threaten Stalin was falsely accused of a crime and arrested. Thousands were executed or sent to prison camps.

Concentration of Power

Kim's first move was to charge his top military commanders with treason. In nationally broadcast trials, he accused more than a dozen top commanders of being American spies. Ten men were publicly executed.

Kim then turned his attention to various splinter groups within the party—mostly the Koreans who had studied in the Soviet Union or others who had fought with Mao. Kim declared that the war had proved which North Koreans were loyal party members and which were traitors. To root out those who were disloyal, he formed a government inspection committee, which was headed by Ho Kai-i.

During the next two years, Ho was responsible for the deaths of more than two-thirds of all party members, a number estimated to be as high as four hundred thousand. Most of the victims were tortured and disfigured. In some cases, the bodies were returned to victims' hometowns and thrown into the central wells there to pollute the local water.

Like Stalin, Kim also established a prison-camp system in the coldest, most remote corner of North Korea. Thousands of disgraced party members—and their extended families—were banished to these camps, where they froze or starved to death. Once Ho had finished doing Kim's dirty work, he, too, went on trial. Ho was accused of weakening the party by killing too many people, and he was publicly executed.

After the Korean War, Kim established prison camps (pictured) in a remote area of North Korea. Thousands of North Koreans who were declared traitors froze or starved to death in these camps.

"Self Reliance"

As the party's ranks were reduced to those who blindly followed Kim, he began to create a unique type of communism. Kim's version mixed the Chinese peasant-based principles with the strong Korean belief in self-reliance.

In 1955, Kim gave a speech in which he criticized the party for being too closely linked to the Soviet Union. He said that instead of dependence, North Koreans should follow the concept he called *juche* (JOO-chay). The literal translation of the word is "self-reliance." The concept comes from a traditional Korean belief that world civilization originated from the Korean peninsula. This concept resulted in a strong nationalistic spirit among Koreans and a fierce hatred of any nation that attempted to control the Korean way of life.

Kim's devoted followers were mainly uneducated peasants who knew little of the history of *juche*, so when Kim claimed that *juche* was his idea, many North Koreans considered it a brilliant and revolutionary thought. Because Korean culture places great importance on veneration of elders, Kim assumed the role of the "father" of *juche*. This made it easy for him to keep all foreign influence at arm's length. From this point on, Kim rarely mentioned communism or referred to either Stalin or Mao. Despite the fact that the North Korean economy was largely supported by the Soviet Union and China, Kim created a perception among North Koreans that they were entirely self-reliant and independent.

Kim's claim to be the originator of *juche* led to one of the most unique forms of political worship in the twentieth century. Some dictators, such as Hitler and Stalin, ruled through fear and lies, and others, like Mao, were considered to be the founder of a new nation and thus deeply revered. No leader, however, received the adoration that Kim did. Newspapers and radios praised Kim as the "iron-willed, ever-victorious commander" and the "respected and beloved Great Leader." North Koreans were taught to think of Kim as the "head and heart" of their nation.

Kim inspired reverence and political adoration in his people that no other dictator had received.

Throughout the 1950s, a cult of personality developed around Kim that seemed strange to outsiders but was accepted by North Koreans, who learned from early childhood on that the "Great Leader" was the "supreme brain of the nation." The Workers' Party was the nerve

69

system that balanced the brain and the body. The masses, of course, were the bone and muscle that carried out all of the commands of the brain and nervous system.

A Closed Society

Once Kim had established himself as the "brain" of North Korea, he began to create a society in which the people followed his will without question. Almost all North Koreans were required to attend study groups and education sessions. There, Kim's thoughts were discussed and his ideology was drilled into participants. The indoctrination was a constant every day fixture, and

A North Korean poster glorifies the masses as the bone and muscle of the nation. The masses were supposed to carry out the brain's, or Kim's, commands.

eventually the majority of North Koreans saw the world the way Kim did.

Kim grouped the population into three classes: the core class, the masses, and the impure class. The core class was about a quarter of the population and consisted of members of the North Korean Workers' Party and those who were descendants of the guerrillas who had fought the Japanese. About half of the population was made up of the masses—workers and peasants. Finally, the members of the impure class were either descendants of the *yangban*, people who cooperated with the Japanese, or North Koreans whose relatives who had fled the country. A person's class influenced virtually every aspect of his or her life, including employment, education, health care, and privileges.

In addition to dividing the population into classes, Kim established housing, travel, and employment controls. Changing one's place of residence was prohibited without party approval, for example. Anyone who moved without permission became ineligible for government benefits and could be arrested. Travel was permitted only with a pass and was limited to official business or family functions. Obtaining a pass often took months, and because the government's system of feeding its citizens and providing health care did not extend to anyone who was traveling, most people never did.

Jobs were assigned by local party officials and had less to do with one's abilities than they did with their political loyalty and class. Job assignments were often illogical. Because Kim required that all men serve in the armed forces, for example, any men who did not serve for health or other reasons were given the most dangerous nonmilitary jobs.

By the late 1950s, villages across the country were organized in the five-family system, which usually consisted of about one hundred people who lived near one another. The group's members chose a chief, generally an elderly person. The chief kept close watch on all the movements and activities of the people in his five-family system. Any deviation from the party line in thought or action was reported to a state security bureau. The chief also held monthly meetings with all of the adults in his five-family system. At these gatherings, discussion usually centered on each person's explanation of what he or she had done to support *juche* in the preceding months.

Kim's government became something like a national *yangban*, the elite class that had been so hated by peasants earlier. The only private ownership allowed was of small garden plots and fruit trees. Some pigs, bees, poultry, and other fowl were allowed to be raised for food, but private gardens could not exceed 160 square

People were allowed to raise livestock and own small plots of land. In all other areas of business and finance, however, the government had complete control.

meters. In truth, farmers were relatively fortunate because of Kim's fond recollection of his father's small farm. In other areas, such as foreign trade, banking, transportation, and communications, the state had total control.

With industry firmly under Kim's thumb, he turned his attention to the North Korean economy and its need to recover from the devastation of the Korean War. To accomplish this, he introduced what he called the Chullima movement. In Korean mythology, Chullima was a flying horse that could run a thousand miles per hour. The idea behind the Chullima movement was that the masses had to work quickly with all their strength to build the economy. Kim also said he wanted "Seeing Stars" workers. By this he meant that they should begin working before dawn—when the stars were out—and not stop working until the stars came out again. Kim's control was so complete that he soon began the "Drink No Soup Movement," which was meant to prevent people from going to the bathroom during work.

For several years, the Chullima movement actually helped the economy of North Korea grow faster than South Korea's. Factories produced heavy machinery such as tractors and trucks, and enough food was produced on state-run farms to also feed industrial workers. Eventually, however, the self-reliance concept hurt North Korea, because most of the industrial and agricultural products of the country were consumed in the country, and there were none to export, which is vital to the health of any nation. Because of this, there were few household consumer goods available to the North Korean population.

The failure to adjust the economy to the world market occurred largely because Kim had little under-standing of the principles of economics. His primary concern was remaining in power and keeping his military strong enough to repel invasion. To achieve these goals, he named people to oversee industries and businesses based on party or personal loyalty. They often had little or no technical knowledge or training and preached to workers about the theories of communism while they sat and watched people work.

By the 1960s, the North Korean economy had begun to lag behind South Korea's. Kim replaced the Chullima movement with other strategies to try to increase industrial production, but with no market to sell their goods, there was no need for more tractors, trucks, or other heavy items. The Changsan idea involved party officials and workers working together to solve problems through discussion and guidance.

The Taean system followed Changsan and required higher-level officials to work side by side with workers. While doing so, Kim declared, the officials should discuss the *juche* ideal, unaware that his insistence on self-reliance was actually harming North Korea.

"Tenderhearted Father"

While Kim continued to urge his people to work harder to build the nation's economy, he privately accumulated vast wealth. By the 1960s, he was living in luxury. He had five palaces around Pyongyang, as well as guesthouses and cottages throughout the country. He was completely cut off from everyone except servants, bodyguards, and carefully selected guests. Even guests, however, were expected to act in specific ways. "There was no such thing as a conversation with Kim," said one servant. "If he spoke to a North Korean, that person stood . . . at attention to receive instruction or orders."[11] No one was allowed to walk on a wide paved road that led from Pyongyang to his main residence. A special lane in the highway was set aside for the exclusive use of his limousine, and no cars but those of the "Great Leader" were permitted on it at any time.

As Kim's power grew, so did his cult of personality. Each article that was written about him in the North Korean press attempted to find new words to describe the "greatness" of the man often called the "tenderhearted father of all the people."[12] During meetings, one aide was assigned to write down every word the "Great Leader" spoke. These were quickly published and distributed among the people to be studied and memorized. "Once said by Kim, it is said forever,"[13] was a common slogan.

Beginning in the 1960s, all North Korean adults were required to wear a badge with Kim's picture on it. More than twenty different Kim badges were designed to be worn by people according to their class or political status. Kim's photograph was on the wall of every home, factory, shop, and office. A house or other location with a dusty or crooked photo of Kim was singled out for criticism at local meetings.

By the end of the 1960s, North Korea had become a nation devoted to Kim. Although he had been a fierce guerrilla fighter, his exploits were exaggerated to the point of ridiculousness. Kim claimed he had fought in more than one hundred thousand battles in fifteen years as a guerrilla—twenty fights a day—and he claimed to have fed his hungry troops by turning sand into rice. Throughout the country, Kim set aside as national monuments famous sites where he had fought, slept, and even sat. In a country where travel was virtually prohibited, citizens were urged to visit all of the shrines devoted to Kim. The only national holiday was April 15, Kim's birthday.

A North Korean's education was based on the thoughts and words of the "Great Leader." More than

As part of his plan to create a nation completely devoted to him, Kim required all North Korean adults to wear a badge with his picture on it.

Students learned every subject with textbooks that centered on Kim. Many of these textbooks even gave incorrect information that credited Kim with discoveries he did not make.

forty thousand Kim Il Sung Revolutionary Thought study rooms were built in North Korea. Education was designed around the subject of Kim from nursery school through college. Textbooks about the Korean language, geography, and science all centered on the words, travels, and discoveries of Kim. While South Korean students received well-rounded educations, North Koreans were taught that Kim had invented both the toaster and the automobile.

Because North Korea was such a closed society, there is no way to know how sincere the devotion to Kim was.

There is little debate, however, that North Korea was rigidly controlled. People were commonly arrested for such offenses as neglecting to wear a Kim badge or unintentionally sitting on a newspaper photo of him. Thousands of people were jailed, tortured, and executed for the slightest break from worship of Kim. The prison-camp system Kim established after the Korean War grew to include twelve camps, with an estimated 150,000 prisoners, many of whom were held for life. In a country with a population of 10 million people, almost everyone knew of a family whose lives had been affected by Kim's security forces.

CHAPTER 5

TENSION AND VIOLENCE

When Kim began his first efforts to rebuild the Korean economy, the nation had some success. By the mid-1960s, however, the tide had turned in favor of South Korea, a country with a population that was three times larger than North Korea's.

Part of the switch was the result of military rule in South Korea that, although strict, resulted in greater stability. The military ruler Park Chung Hee believed that for South Korea's economy to grow, it needed the help of American-trained economists. Park also began to build strong trade relations with Japan and the United States.

Failing Economy

North Korea, on the other hand, continued to reject trade relationships with other nations, and Kim did not seek advice from outside economics experts; instead, he relied on his own judgment. Throughout his many years in power, Kim traveled around North Korea to make surprise visits to factories and farms to give advice. News reports often told of Kim telling farmers to plant rice at a time he felt would bring a larger crop (instead of at the usual time). North Korean reporters would write

Kim often visited factories and farms to give advice and refused to turn to outside economic experts even when North Korea's economy suffered.

that the advice of the "Great Leader" resulted in the largest crop in history, when, in fact, the crop had failed.

Because much of what Kim said was considered almost divine by North Koreans, few people dared to challenge his advice. Government officials were forced to resign if they suggested ideas that were counter to Kim's. "Nobody was allowed to change anything," said a North Korean official who fled the country. "The smallest sign of deviation means the system has developed a dangerous crack."[14]

Military Buildup

In addition to a reliance on Kim's economic direction, another major strain on North Korea's economic well-being was the amount spent on its armed forces. By the late 1960s, when South Korea was spending less than 5 percent of its budget on defense, North Korea was devoting more than 20 percent of its budget for the same purpose. Throughout North Korea, the tightly controlled media convinced the people that the nation was in constant danger of attack. "We are always making preparations for war," Kim once said. "We do not conceal this matter."[15]

Kim did succeed in creating a strong military. In the 1960s, he established the so-called Four Great Military

Lines as a national policy. Under these guidelines, all citizens are armed, the entire country is fortified, each soldier is capable of taking command, and all equipment is the most modern that is available.

By the late 1960s, the North Korean army had more than four hundred thousand active troops, making it the fourth largest standing army among Communist nations. In addition, Kim built a substantial air force and navy from ships and planes supplied by the Soviet Union and China. U.S. intelligence officials described the North Korean army as an "efficient, well-trained, and highly disciplined fighting force."[16]

By the late 1960s, North Korea spent more than 20 percent of its budget on defense and had the fourth largest army among Communist nations.

Of the twenty-three divisions in the North Korean army, fourteen of them, about three hundred thousand troops, were stationed along the demilitarized zone (DMZ). On the other side of the DMZ, more than two hundred thousand South Korean and American troops held their ground, backed up by as many as a hundred nuclear missiles.

Many people considered the DMZ one of the most dangerous places on Earth and a location where war could easily break out. Kim blamed the United States for the tension that existed between the two countries. To keep his people on guard against attack, he accused the United States of "carrying out war drills and importing weapons to South Korea."[17] Meanwhile, Kim's intelligence agents slipped into South Korea to spy on U.S. and South Korean forces. North Korean spies created still more tension when they made two assassination attempts on South Korean politicians in the 1960s and instigated student revolts against the South Korean military rulers.

A Brief Opening

In April 1972, Kim celebrated his sixtieth birthday, the age at which a person is officially recognized as an elder in Korean culture. To mark the occasion, the ninety-two

Dedicated to Kim, the Museum of Revolution (pictured) opened in April 1972 in honor of the leader's sixtieth birthday.

room Museum of the Revolution, which was dedicated to Kim, had its opening. Nearby, a sixty-six-foot gilded statue of the "Great Leader" was unveiled—the largest statue of a Korean ever erected.

Despite the nation's deep economic troubles, Kim's power remained secure. His one unfulfilled wish, however, was for the two nations on the Korean peninsula to reunite —preferably as a Communist state under his control. With his usual self-confidence, he decided the time was right to open talks with South Korea. In May 1972, Kim met a delegate from South Korea to discuss reunification.

In September a delegation of North Koreans, each wearing a Kim Il Sung badge, walked across the DMZ and into South Korea in what was the first peaceful visit to that nation by North Koreans since before the Korean War. Although the meeting did not result in any solid agreements, it was the first step taken by North Korea to reach out to the world.

Also during 1972 the United States opened relations with China and the Soviet Union. North Korea, which had heavily depended on aid from them, realized it could not continue to rely solely on Communist financial support. North Korea's effort to establish diplomatic relations with South Korea caught the world's attention. Within a year, the number of countries that had diplomatic relations with North Korea rose from thirty-one—all Communist—to ninety-three. North Korea also established diplomatic relations with the United States for the first time. In an effort to prop himself up psychologically, Kim promoted himself from premier to president for life—a title he thought elevated him above the leaders of South Korea and the United States.

Trouble Returns

Unfortunately for the Korean people, the reduction in tensions did not last. Political unrest in South Korea and

North Korean efforts to exacerbate it provoked a return to mutual mistrust.

The South Korean military leadership had created a great deal of discontent in its society, despite economic progress. Students and Christian groups led violent protests against the military's strict rule. In some cases,

When South Korean students, who often protested their country's military government, began to support communism, many thought Kim was behind an effort to undermine South Korea's political structure.

student organizations expressed support for communism, and many South Koreans suspected North Korean agents of fomenting rebellion.

Tensions increased in August 1974, when an assassination attempt was made on South Korean president Park Chung Hee during a speech. Park's wife and a bystander were killed in the attempt. The assassin was captured and was soon revealed to have been trained by North Korean intelligence officers.

To make matters worse, three months after the assassination attempt, South Korean troops on patrol in the DMZ discovered an elaborate system of tunnels. U.S. and South Korean troops converged on the area and eventually found more than twenty tunnels. Most of them began a mile or two behind the North Korean lines and ended a mile into South Korea. Several were big enough to allow an estimated ten thousand soldiers per hour to pass under the DMZ and emerge in South Korean territory.

During their search, the South Koreans captured a North Korean spy who said the tunnels had been dug for years on Kim's orders. During peacetime, they were a passageway for intelligence agents, and if war broke out, they would permit North Korean infantry to stage a surprise rear attack. The fact that Kim had ordered the tunnels to be dug at the same time he had signed an agreement with South Korean leaders "not to undertake . . . provocations against one another" convinced South Korean and American leaders that he could not be trusted.[18]

Suspicions that Kim was attempting to undermine South Korean political stability resulted in an intense military buildup of South Korean and American forces at the DMZ. In addition to the arrival of thousands of American soldiers, the United States sent its most advanced fighter planes and nuclear-armed bombers to South Korea in a show of force. The buildup continued into the summer of 1976, when the combined U.S. and South Korean forces staged Operation Team Spirit, massive military exercises intended to show the North Koreans what they would face if they invaded. Operation Team Spirit sent a wave of panic through North Korea, and Kim declared that the South Koreans and Americans planned to "directly ignite the fuse of war."[19]

Relations between the two Koreas grew even more strained in August when American soldiers who were ordered to cut down an enormous tree directly on the DMZ line were confronted by a patrol of North Koreans. Angry words were exchanged, and the North Koreans attacked with fists and clubs. Two American officers were beaten to death, and four others were seriously injured. Tension rose to a level that was almost as high as at the end of the Korean War.

Within days, the Korean peninsula was on the verge of all-out war. American ships were sent to Korean waters, heavy artillery and tanks were put into place on the South Korean side of the DMZ, and U.S. attack helicopters were readied for action. The North Korean leadership, as well as Kim, realized that the killings were a dangerous mistake. Despite the fact that Kim had expanded his army to more than seven hundred thousand troops, it was no match for the modern weaponry arrayed against it.

Several days after the killings, another U.S. work detail was sent to cut down the tree. Guarded by thousands of troops, with attack helicopters and jet fighters flying overhead, the tree was quickly removed. For his part, Kim said the deaths were "regretful" and claimed that the Americans had started the fight. Kim was proven wrong when a film of the incident showed otherwise.

Loss of Support

Despite the fact that war was avoided in the mid-1970s, Kim's actions still had a negative impact on North Korea. His main sources of military and economic aid, China and the Soviet Union, began to withdraw

THE CHINESE–SOVIET SPLIT

Although feelings between the Communist leaderships of China and the Soviet Union had never been warm, by the late 1960s, the two nations had become bitter enemies. China's leader Mao Tse-tung had never forgiven Soviet premier Joseph Stalin for breaking a promise to help Chinese and North Korean forces in the Korean War.

Events after Stalin's death in 1953 widened the gulf between the two countries. The new Soviet leader, Nikita Khrushchev, angered the Chinese when he dropped Stalin's strategy of all-out war with Western powers in favor of what he called "peaceful coexistence." Mao, however, was deeply convinced that war between communism and the West was necessary for a world Communist government.

Personally, Khrushchev and Mao intensely disliked each other. Khrushchev often refused Mao's requests for assistance in the 1950s when the new Chinese economy struggled. When aid was forthcoming, it came at a cost Mao felt violated his Communist principles. He disliked his dependence on a Communist nation such as the Soviet Union that advocated peaceful coexistence.

Khrushchev also went to great lengths to rid the Soviet Union of the cult of personality that had formed around Stalin. Mao, who disliked Stalin, had his own cult of personality in China, and he resented Khrushchev's implied criticisms of his leadership style.

A significant contributor to tension between the two Communist giants was the fact that the Soviet Union and China were in different stages of development. China, which formed its Communist government in 1949, was in the earliest stage of development. The Soviets, on the other hand, had been in power for more than forty years.

The rift between both countries deepened when China became the second Communist nation with nuclear weapons. Mao felt that having the weapons allowed him to pursue a global Communist revolution because the United States would not challenge him. Khrushchev felt that possessing nuclear weapons gave the Soviet Union security from attack and allowed it to develop mutually beneficial relations with capitalist countries.

Even after Khrushchev left office in the mid-1960s, relations between China and the Soviet Union continued to be strained, and in 1969, the two nations fought several skirmishes across their four-thousand-mile border. Eventually, the hostilities ceased, but the split between the two countries was never healed.

Chinese vice premier Bo Yibo and U.S. president Jimmy Carter signed agreements that opened trade relations between their countries in 1980. As relations between China and the United States improved, Kim could no longer depend on China for support.

support. By this time, the two Communist giants were bitter enemies because of disagreements about which country followed true Communist principles. They had both opened trade relations with the United States, and Cold War tensions between the three diminished.

For most of his years in power, Kim had found a way to remain on good terms with both China and the Soviet Union without taking a side in their dispute. Both nations, however, were alarmed by the events in the DMZ and began to see Kim as a loose cannon who could hurt their attempts to build relations with the West.

China, which had provided most of North Korea's oil and natural gas at almost no cost, reduced the amount it supplied, and, at the same time, raised prices. The Soviet Union, which had supported North Korea with billions of dollars of aid and loans since 1953, cut back as well. The Soviets also requested that the loans be repaid, which North Korea was unable to do.

The Chinese turned down Kim's request for technical assistance in the development of nuclear weapons. (China had the atomic bomb since the 1960s.) Soviet leaders declined when Kim asked for their latest jet fighters—the only such rebuff the Soviets made to any Communist ally. Both countries believed that Kim would use the weaponry to attack South Korea.

The difficulties Kim created for his country were unknown to most North Koreans, who believed the "Great Leader" when he promised in each New Year's address that North Koreans would soon be able to "eat rice and meat soup, wear silk clothes, and live in a tile roofed house."[20]

CHAPTER 6

FAILURE IN THE FINAL YEARS

In 1981, on the eve of Kim's seventieth birthday, North Korea's economic problems had led to famine in rural areas and near bankruptcy, yet the media continued to glorify the "Great Leader" with praise. A newspaper declared, "Kim Il Sung . . . is the great father of our people. . . . Father—this familiar word represents our people's single heart of boundless respect and loyalty. . . . The love shown by the Great Leader for our people is the love of kinship. . . . His heart . . . [attracts] the hearts of all people. . . . [Thanks] to this great heart, national independence is firmly guaranteed."[21]

Kim knew he could not remain in power forever, and in 1981, he publicly announced that his son, Kim Jong Il, would become president when his father died. Kim Jong Il, who had no political or military experience and who had grown up in seclusion, was soon referred to as "Dear Leader" in the press. To provide his son with leadership experience, Kim placed him in charge of North Korean intelligence.

The Seoul Olympics

While the younger Kim ran the well-established intelligence bureau in North Korea, his father's inability to manage the economy made conditions worse throughout North Korea in the 1980s. Meanwhile, many of the political and economic problems faced by South Korea had dissipated. In fact, by the early 1980s, South Korea had the second largest

In 1980, Kim Il Sung (left) announced that, when he died, his son Kim Jong Il (right) would become president.

By the 1980s, Seoul (pictured) was a thriving modern metropolis and South Korea had the second largest economy in Asia. North Korea's economy, in contrast, was near bankruptcy.

economy in Asia (Japan's was the biggest). Seoul had become one of the most modern cities in Asia, and South Korean leaders were eager to find a way to showcase the nation's success.

South Korean political and business teachers made an application to host the 1988 Olympic Games in Seoul. When the International Olympic Committee awarded the games to Seoul, it focused international attention on both Koreas. The international community, as well as Communist countries whose economies were collapsing due to the failure of their economic models began to see South Korea as a promising trading partner.

Nations that North Korea depended upon for assistance, such as China and the Soviet Union, established trade relations with Pyongyang's bitter enemy. Smaller Communist nations, including Hungary and East Germany, which had been under the control of the Soviet Union, also began to trade with South Korea.

North Korean leaders realized that the Olympic Games offered an opportunity to open relations with non-Communist countries—and perhaps to steal some of the attention that was falling on South Korea. The North Koreans were also deeply concerned that their Communist allies were turning away from them in favor of South Korea. In 1986, North Korean delegates approached the Olympic Committee and tried to hijack the games by demanding that Olympic events be divided evenly between Seoul and Pyongyang. South Korea objected but did offer to let two competitions be held in Pyongyang. North Korea refused the offer.

When Seoul won the opportunity to host the 1988 Olympic Games, Kim tried to create doubt about the locale's safety.

97

North Koreans, enraged that they had lost international respect, sought to sow doubts that Seoul was a safe location for the games. Kim and his son devised a plan they believed would instill fear among countries that would be sending athletes to compete. In November 1987, a North Korean man and woman boarded a South Korean airliner in Baghdad, Iraq, planted a bomb on board, and got off the plane at its next stop. The bomb exploded while the plane was en route to Seoul and killed 115 people, mostly South Korean men who were on their way home from jobs in Middle Eastern oil fields.

The terrorist attack shocked the world. Shock turned to fury when police arrested the two bombers. The man committed suicide before he could be questioned, but the woman admitted her guilt and said she had acted at Kim Il Sung's direction. "It was a military order," she told investigators, "to be accepted without question."[22]

In the end, the bombing did little to discourage nations from participating in the Olympics, but it did do enormous damage to the reputation of North Korea and its "Great Leader," who were considered international outlaws. In late September 1988, the athletes of more than 160 nations marched into Olympic stadium in Seoul. Among them were China, the Soviet Union, and all the Communist nations with the exception of North Korea.

The games were broadcast in virtually every country of the world, except North Korea.

The Fall of Communism

The loss of international respect for North Korea over the bombing was the first in a series of disasters that befell Communist nations. By the end of the 1980s, Communist governments around the world began to collapse. The Soviet Union broke up into Russia and several other nations. Although China remained Communist, its leaders permitted the creation of private businesses and developed trade relations with South Korea and other Asian nations.

For North Korea, the fall of communism was a disaster. Both Russia and China began to demand payment for assistance provided to Pyongyang because they were not financially stable enough to continue extending credit to North Korea as they had done in the past. North Korea's energy imports were cut in half, which meant that there was no fuel for construction machinery, factories, or motor vehicles.

Even worse for the North Koreans were continued food shortages that plagued the countryside. Starvation became a threat in more remote areas. Hundreds of thousands of people were reduced to eating soup made of rice and grass. Reports of cannibalism began to be heard in the West. It is now estimated that a million people starved to death in the early 1990s.

As Kim approached eighty, North Korea had become his own personal monument. The few visitors to North Korea found Pyongyang to be unlike any large city they had ever encountered. The roads that led into the capital were empty, and streets and sidewalks were not crowded, partly because elderly, disabled, and sick people were forced to leave.

In addition to the enormous gilded statue of Kim in Pyongyang, was a monument to the concept of *juche* that was taller than the Washington Monument. In the center of the city was the hundred-thousand-seat Kim Il Sung Stadium, which was used only for mass demonstrations of loyalty to Kim or his son. Nearby was a 105-story hotel, which was the tallest in Asia but contained construction flaws so dangerous that it was never occupied.

Death of the "Great Leader"

Whether Kim realized the damage he had done to his people is unknown. In his annual New Year's speech in 1994, Kim acknowledged for the first time that the people of North Korea faced "considerable difficulties and obstacles," and that the situation in which the country found itself was "complicated and strained."[23]

Even then, however, Kim continued to exert his power. Although he had turned over day-to-day decisions to his son, Kim continued to travel around the country to factories and farms. In June 1994, he visited seventeen collective farms and factories, offering advice on how to increase harvests or production at each stop.

On July 7, Kim made a surprise stop at a collective farm near his favorite palace outside Pyongyang. Although the temperature was nearly one hundred degrees, the "Great Leader" walked through the fields and offered suggestions that were copied down by aides. That evening at dinner in the palace, Kim complained that he felt tired. A few hours later, he collapsed and died from a massive heart attack.

Kim's death was kept secret for two days while arrangements were made for the shift of power to Kim Jong Il. On July 9, North Koreans watched a special announcement on TV. The announcer described Kim in the usual terms: "Our respected fatherly leader who has devoted his whole life to the popular masses' cause of independence . . . and happiness . . . [has] departed from us to our great sorrow."[24]

Throughout the day, thousands of weeping North Koreans gathered at the enormous statue of Kim in

Although Kim Il Sung led North Korea into economic ruin and caused the deaths of millions, thousands of people still pay their respects at the mausoleum of the "Great Leader" each day.

Pyongyang. Hospitals overflowed with people who had suffered heart attacks upon hearing the news. The following week, a memorial ceremony was held for Kim Il Sung in the stadium that bore his name.

Kim Jong Il appeared before the crowd at the stadium, announced as "Dear Leader," the sole successor to the "Great Leader." Unlike his father, who was a large man with a deep, rumbling voice, the younger Kim was small with curly hair. At the long ceremony, some party officials read from the writings of the "Great Leader." While others praised Kim, Kim Jong Il, who was difficult to see among the dignitaries on stage, did not speak.

By 1994, Kim had ruled North Korea for forty-six years. He had come to power when the country was being rebuilt after the devastation of World War II. In 1950, Kim brought more destruction by beginning the Korean War, during which 3 million Koreans were killed. For more than forty years, he led his people deeper and deeper into economic ruin and starved more than a million people to death. His rule had caused the deaths of millions and nearly started a nuclear war. It is easy to understand why American president Bill Clinton, looking across the DMZ to North Korea in 1994, called it "the scariest place on Earth."[25]

CHRONOLOGY

1912	Kim Song ju is born.
1930	Kim Il Sung is released from jail and joins a Korean Independence Army unit.
1936	Japanese newspapers depict Kim Il Sung as a "bandit" preying upon poor Korean farmers.
1937	Kim's unit defeats Japanese forces at Pochonbo.
1939–1945	World War II.
1941	Kim becomes part of the 88th Special Brigade of the Soviet Army.
1942	Kim fights at Stalingrad; Kim Jong Il is born.
1945	Kim receives a hero's welcome at the Pyongyang Municipal Stadium.
1948	The Democratic People's Republic of North Korea is founded; Kim is named premier.
1950	North Korea invades South Korea.
1953	Cease-fire begins after the Korean War; the DMZ is established.

1955	Kim describes *juche*, the ideal of self-reliance for North Korean economy
1968	Kim signs a nonaggression agreement with South Korea
1974	North Korean tunnels are discovered under the DMZ.
1976	North Korean soldiers kill two American soldiers in the DMZ.
1987	Kim approves the bombing of a Korean airlines flight; 115 South Koreans are killed.
1994	Kim dies and his son takes his place as North Korea's leader.

GLOSSARY

capitalism Economic system based on private ownership.

communism Political system in which there is no
private property.

cult Group of people devoted to a person or idea.

dictator A person with absolute power in a society.

economy A nation's production, distribution, and
consumption of goods and services.

elite A social class with great power and influence.

famine An extreme shortage of food.

guerrilla An independent fighter not part of a regular
army unit.

nationalist A person who is strongly devoted to his or
her country.

socialism Belief that communism's revolution will be
attained by natural and peaceful progression.

Source Notes

Introduction: "We Must Wipe Out the Traitors"

1. Quoted in Young Sik Kim, *Eyewitness: A North Korean Remembers*, Korea Web Weekly, 1995. http://kimsoft.com/korea/eyewit.htm.

2. Quoted in Bruce Cumings, "An Exchange on Korean War Origins," CWIHP Bulletin, Woodrow Wilson Institute for Strategic Studies, July 11, 1995. http://wwics.si.edu.

Chapter 1: Early Years

3. Don Oberdorfer, *Two Koreas*. New York: Basic Books, 2001, p. xv.

4. Kim Il Sung, *With the Century*, Korea Web Weekly, ch. 1.1. www.kimsoft.com/war/w-r-0.htm.

5. Kim Il Sung, *With the Century*, ch. 1.7.

Chapter 2: Bandit and Officer

6. Kim Il Sung, *With the Century*, ch. 3.10.

7. Quoted in Oberdorfer, *Two Koreas*, p. 17.

8. Kim Il Sung, *With the Century*, ch. 24.8.

Chapter 3: The Korean Conflict

9. Quoted in Young Sik Kim, *Eyewitness*.

10. Quoted in Young Sik Kim, *Eyewitness*.

Chapter 4: The Brain of the People

11. Quoted in Oberdorfer, *Two Koreas*, p. 19.

12. Andrea Matles Savada, ed., "Corporatism and the Chuch'e Idea," *North Korea: A Country Study*. Library of Congress, June 1993. http://lcweb2.loc.gov/frd/cs/kptoc.html.

13. Oberdorfer, *Two Koreas*, p. 21.

Chapter 5: Tension and Violence

14. Quoted in Savada, *North Korea*.

15. Quoted in Oberdorfer, *Two Koreas*, p. 22.

16. Quoted in Oberdorfer, *Two Koreas*, p. 61.

17. Oberdorfer, *Two Koreas*, p. 22.

18. Quoted in Oberdorfer, *Two Koreas*, p. 25.

19. Quoted in Oberdorfer, *Two Koreas*, p. 61.

20. Oberdorfer, *Two Koreas*, p. 298.

Chapter 6: Failure in the Final Years

21. Quoted in Savada, *North Korea*.

22. Quoted in Oberdorfer, *Two Koreas*, p. 185.

23. Oberdorfer, *Two Koreas*, p. 342.

24. Quoted in Oberdorfer, *Two Koreas*, p. 343.

25. Quoted in Oberdorfer, *Two Koreas*, p. 345.

For More Information

Books

William Dudley, *North and South Korea*. San Diego, CA: Greenhaven, 2002.

Valerie Hill, *Ask About Asia: Korea*. Toronto, Canada: Mason Crest, 2002.

Christopher Salter, *Modern World Nations: North Korea*. Broomall, PA: Chelsea House, 2003.

Websites

Eyewitness: A North Korean Remembers (http://kimsoft.com/korea/eyewit.htm). An extensive Web-based historical biography with direct source material.

North Korea: A Country Study (http://lcweb2.loc.gov/frd/cs/kptoc.html). One of the most complete studies of North Korean history and culture. The site was developed by the Library of Congress.

INDEX

Picture Credits

Cover, pages 33, 37, 45, 60, 73, 85, 87, 97 © Corbis

pages 5, 6, 8, 19, 77, 83, 95, 102 © AFP/Getty Images

page 10 © PhotoDisc

pages 14, 17, 24, 31, 42, 47, 50, 67, 69, 81, 92 © Hulton|Archive by Getty Images

pages 21, 23 © Library of Congress

page 27 © Hulton-Deutsch Collection/Corbis

pages 29, 49 © Bettmann/Corbis

pages 40, 58, 61, 63 © National Archives

page 70 © Tony Wheeler/Lonely Planet Images

page 78 © Reuters/Landov

page 96 © Corel